Audio Access Included

PIANO SOLO

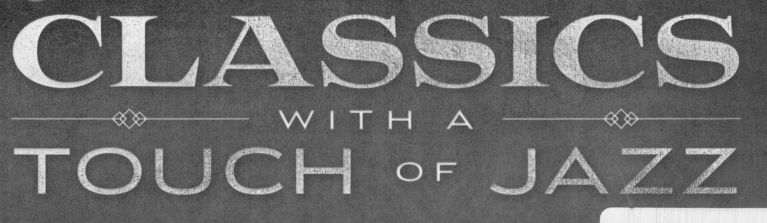

CLASSICS

⬥⬥ WITH A ⬥⬥

TOUCH OF JAZZ

27 BELOVED MASTERPIECES
ARRANGED BY
LEE EVANS

To MARK PORTER, who planted the seed of this book

To access audio visit:
www.halleonard.com/mylibrary

4107-8565-4266-8931

ISBN 978-1-4950-4733-6

HAL•LEONARD®
CORPORATION
7777 W. Bluemound Rd. P.O. Box 13819 Milwaukee, WI 53213

In Australia Contact:
Hal Leonard Australia Pty. Ltd.
4 Lentara Court
Cheltenham, Victoria, 3192 Australia
Email: ausadmin@halleonard.com.au

Visit Hal Leonard Online at
www.halleonard.com

PREFACE

Classics with a Touch of Jazz is a reflection of my long-standing interest in keeping music students and their teachers motivated through the inclusion of jazz music and concepts within the traditional classical piano lesson.

I grew up as a classically-trained pianist and an avid listener of classical music. I also spent eight years in high school and college performing standard symphonic literature on my second instrument, the double bass, first taught to me in NYC's amazing High School of Music & Art. These experiences—added to my many years as jazz pianist and author—have allowed me to comfortably explore a marvelous manifestation of my liberal musical outlook: the writing of piano solo transcriptions of well-known classical repertoire, with jazz touches.

My work in this area was inspired by Franz Liszt, the towering 19th century composer and pianist. His passion for transcribing other composers' music—songs, operatic excerpts, symphonies (including all nine of Beethoven's)—into brilliant and compelling piano fantasies and paraphrases is inspiring and infectious.

I recorded each piece to provide a useful model for practice and performance. The recordings are accessible online with the special code printed on the title page. My fervent hope is that the fresh jazz approach of this volume will result in heightened student motivation, as well as renewed interest in our incomparable western classical-music heritage.

Lee Evans

CONTENTS

PIANO SONATA NO. 16
K. 545, 2nd Movement Theme

WOLFGANG AMADEUS MOZART
Arranged by LEE EVANS

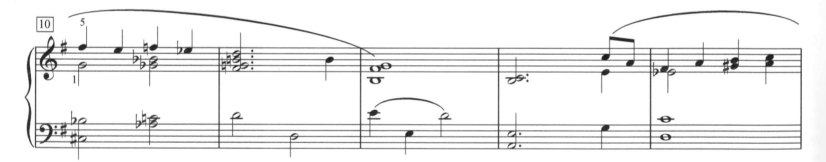

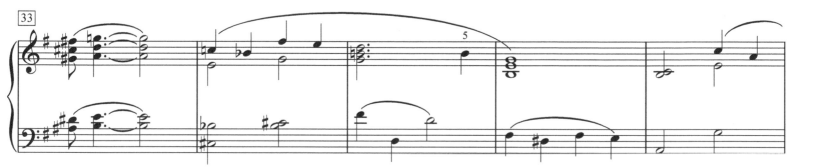

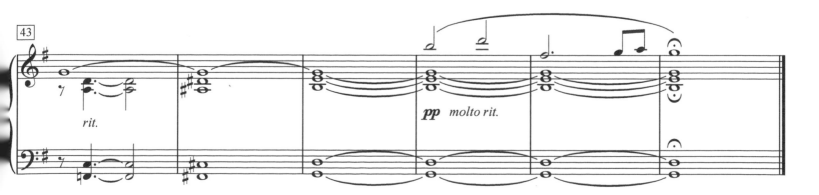

5

PAVANE
Op. 50

GABRIEL FAURÉ
Arranged by LEE EVANS

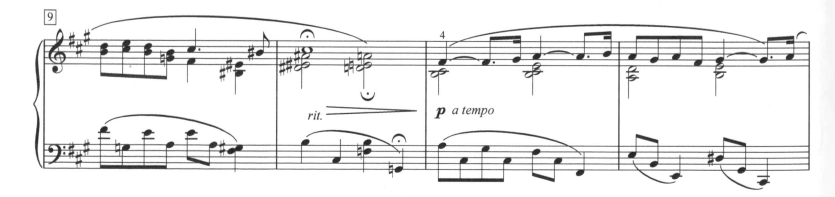

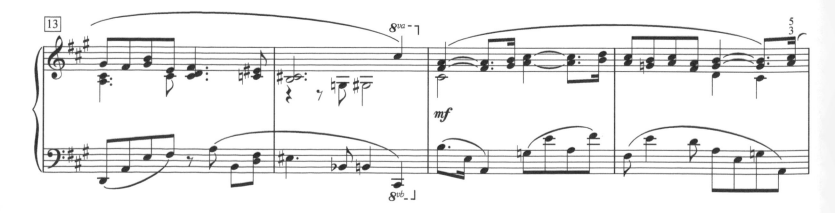

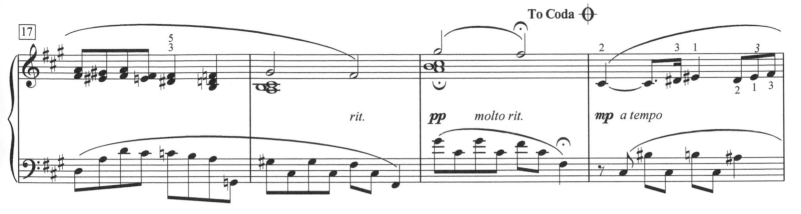

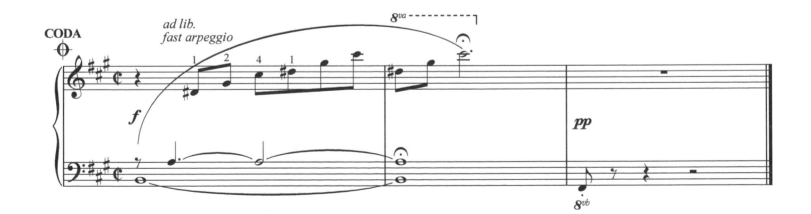

TRÄUMEREI
Op. 15, No. 7

ROBERT SCHUMANN
Arranged by LEE EVANS

Expressively

p

With pedal

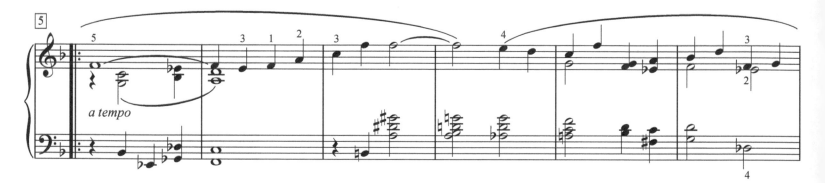

a tempo

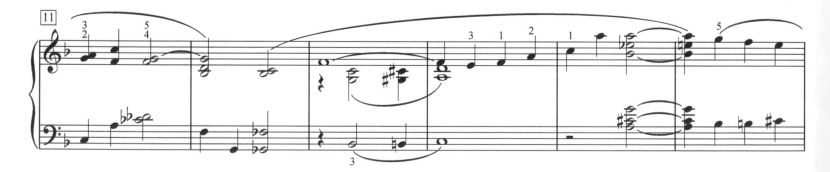

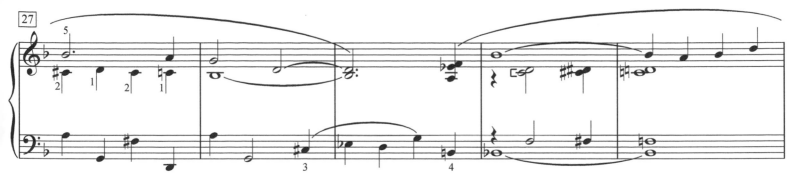

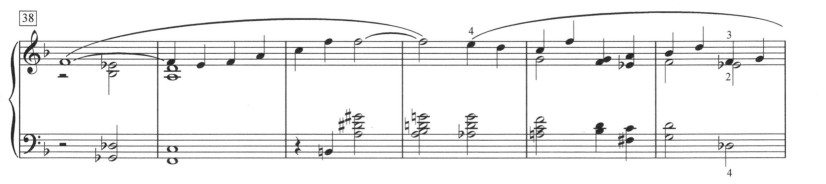

AIR FROM ORCHESTRAL SUITE NO. 3
BWV 1068

JOHANN SEBASTIAN BACH
Arranged by LEE EVANS

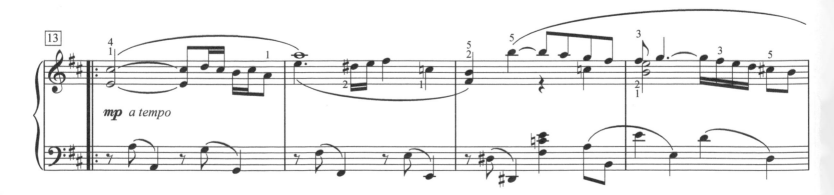

PIANO SONATA NO. 8
"Pathétique", Op. 13, 2nd Movement Theme

LUDWIG VAN BEETHOVEN
Arranged by LEE EVANS

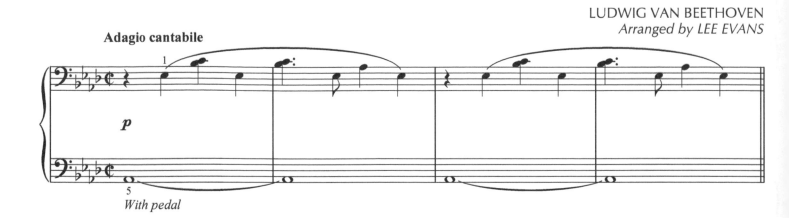

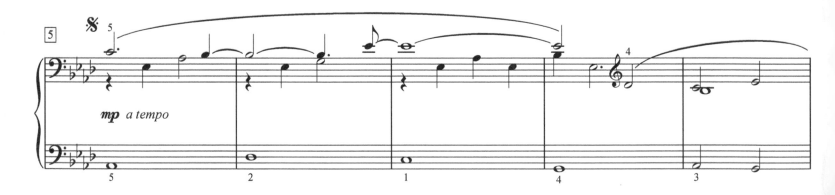

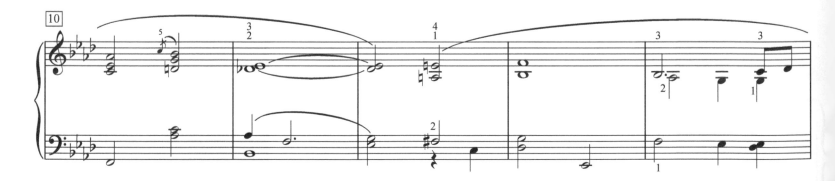

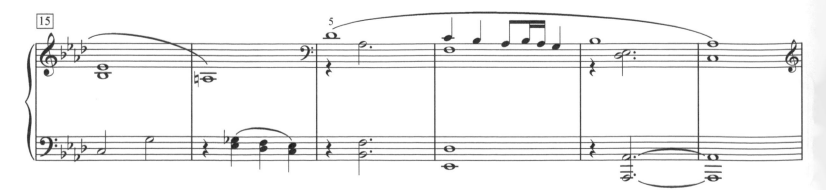

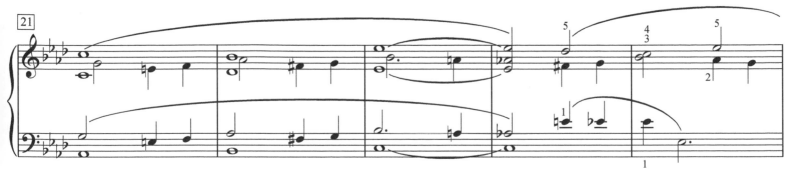

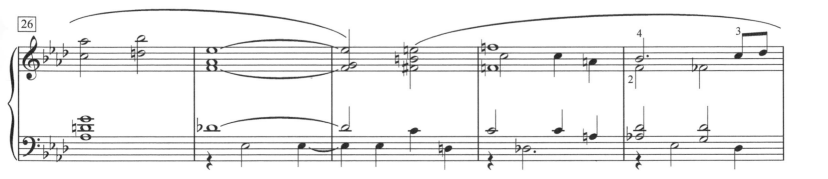

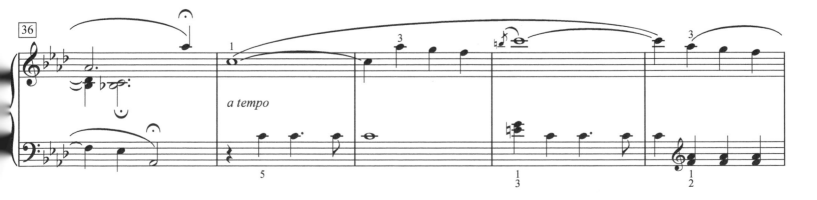

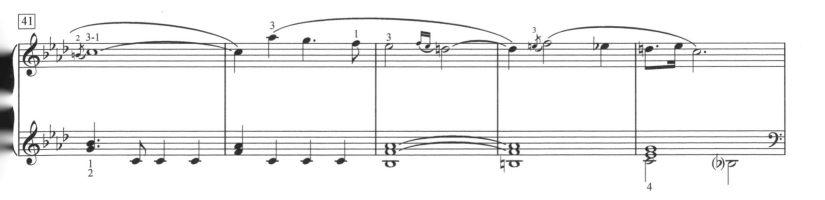

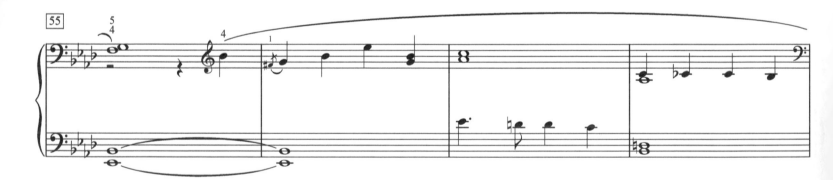

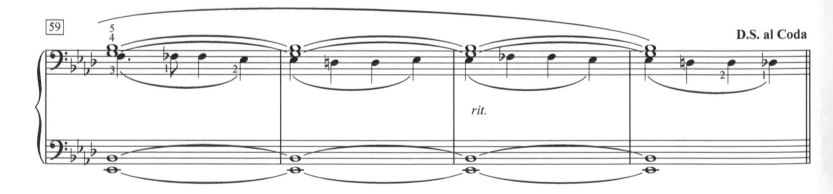

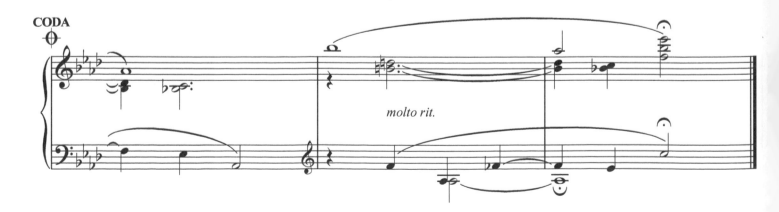

PAVANE DE LA BELLE AU BOIS DORMANT

(Sleeping Beauty Pavane)
from MOTHER GOOSE SUITE

MAURICE RAVEL
Arranged by LEE EVANS

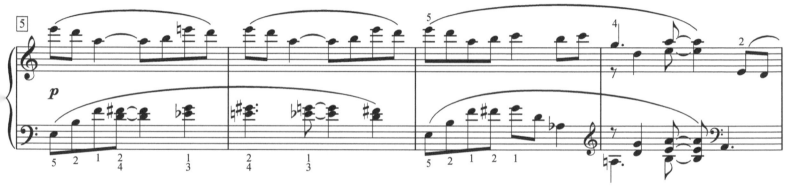

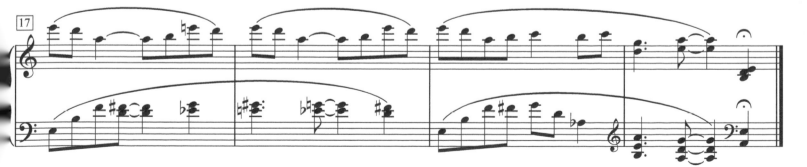

LES ENTRETIENS DE LA BELLE ET DE LA BETE
(Conversations Between Beauty and the Beast)
from MOTHER GOOSE SUITE

MAURICE RAVEL
Arranged by LEE EVANS

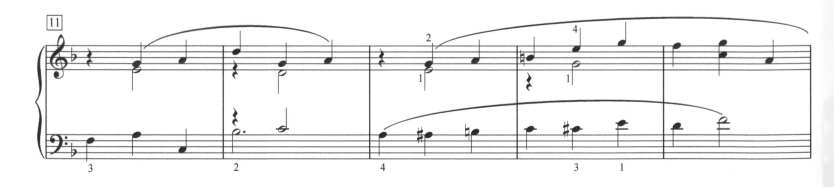

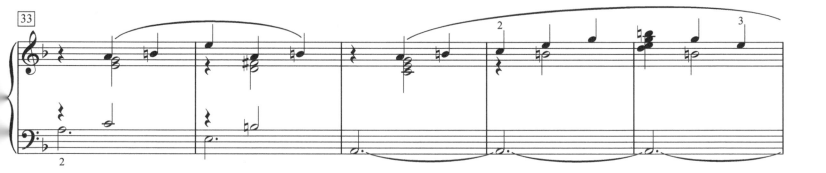

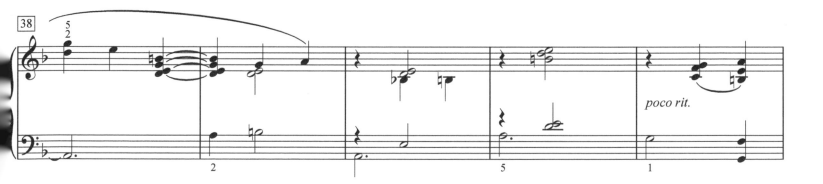

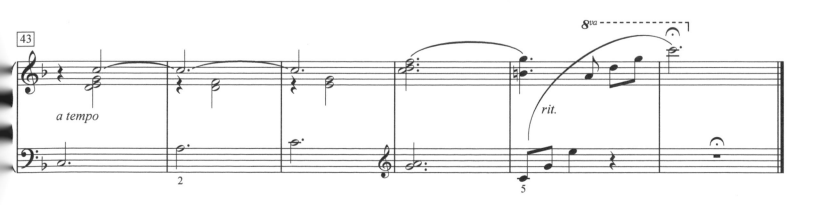

SICILIENNE
Op. 78

GABRIEL FAURÉ
Arranged by LEE EVANS

Brightly

With light pedal

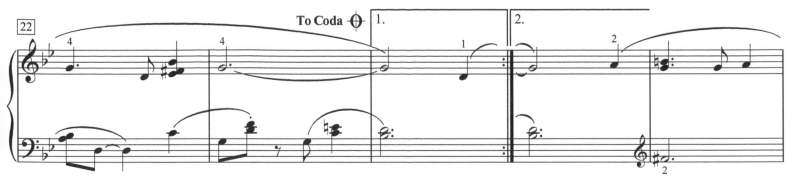

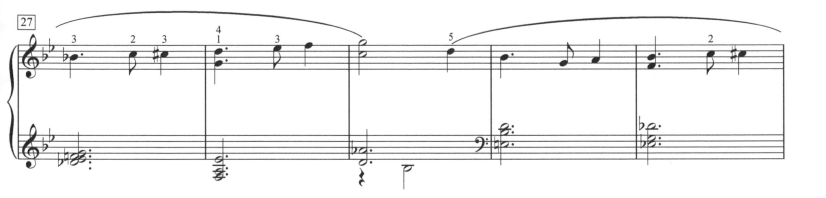

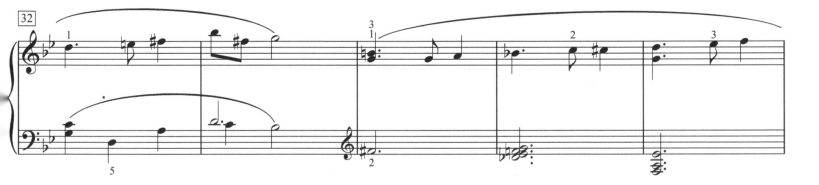

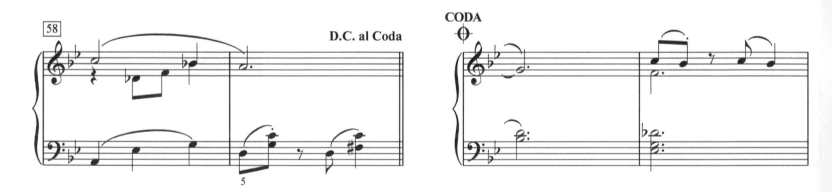

D.C. al Coda

CODA

REVERIE

CLAUDE DEBUSSY
Arranged by LEE EVANS

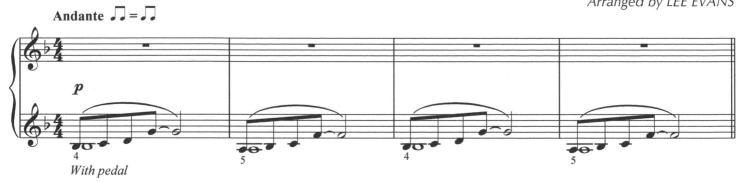

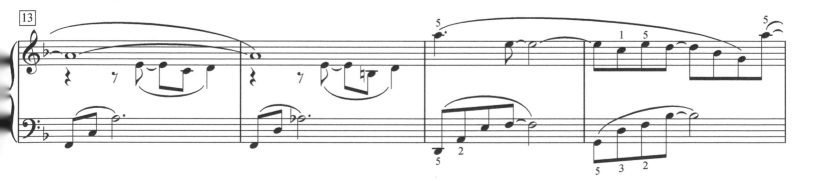

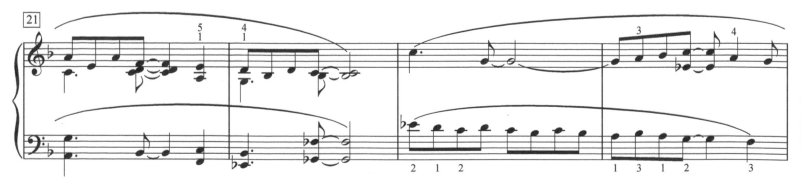

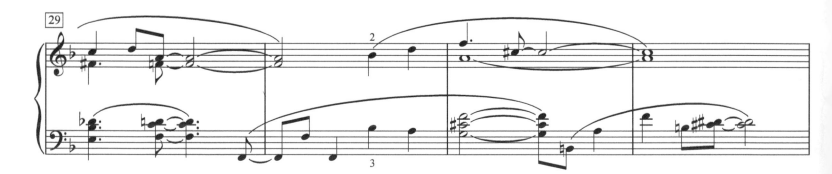

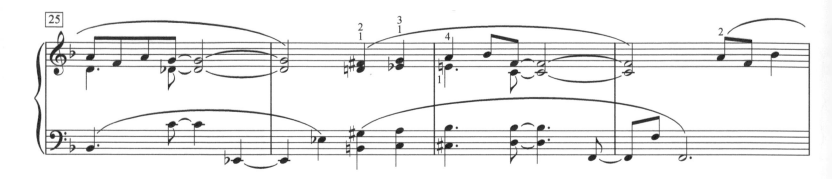

To Coda ⊕

rit.

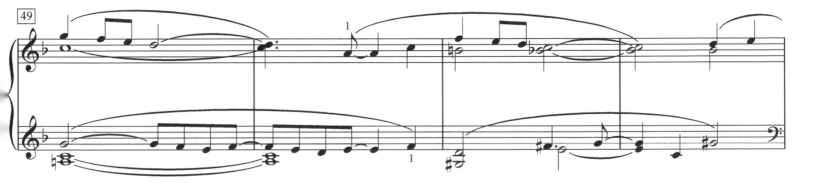

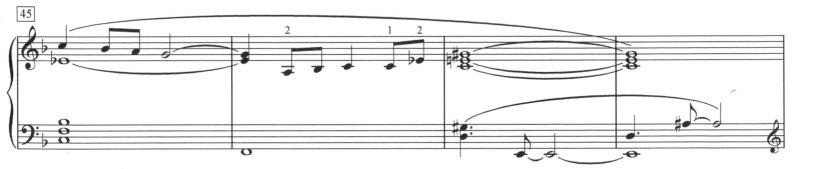

D.S. al Coda

OBOE CONCERTO
2nd Movement Theme

ALESSANDRO MARCELLO
Arranged by LEE EVANS

Adagio; molto rubato

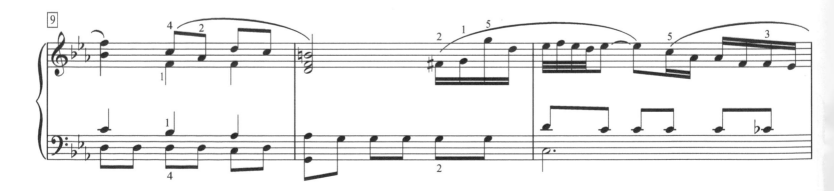

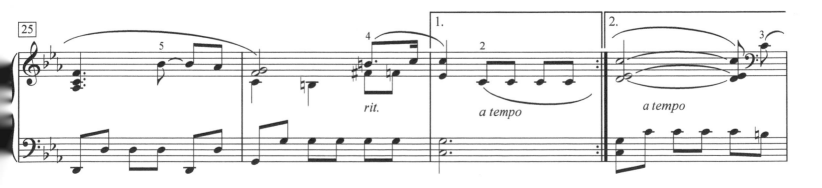

PIANO SONATA NO. 11

K. 331, 1st Movement Theme

WOLFGANG AMADEUS MOZART
Arranged by LEE EVANS

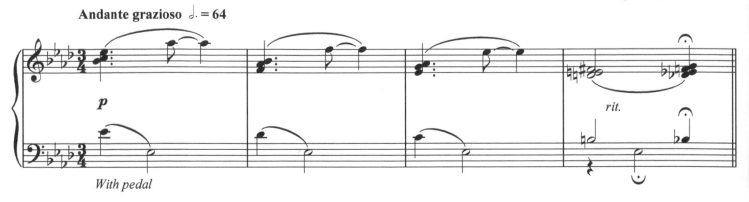

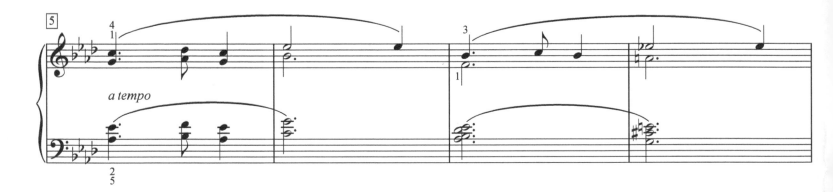

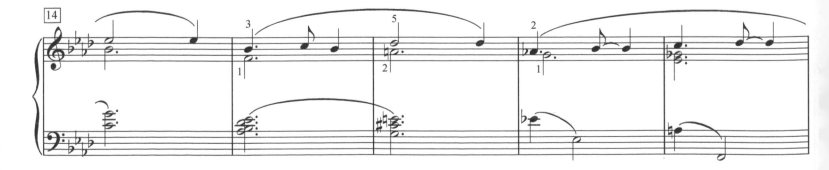

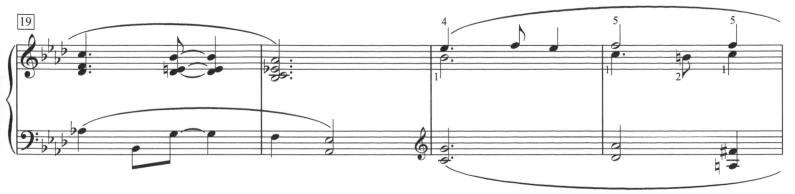

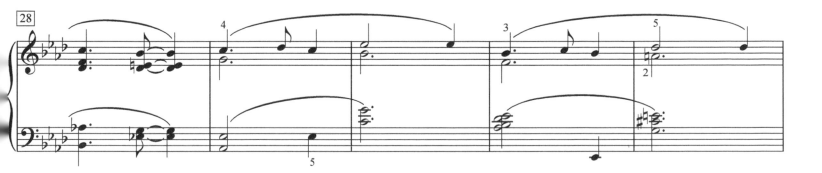

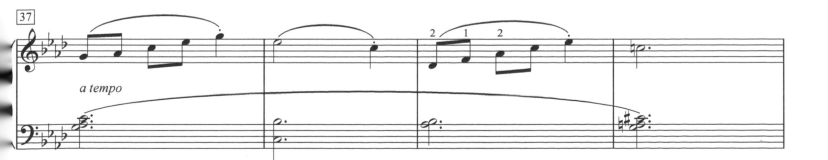

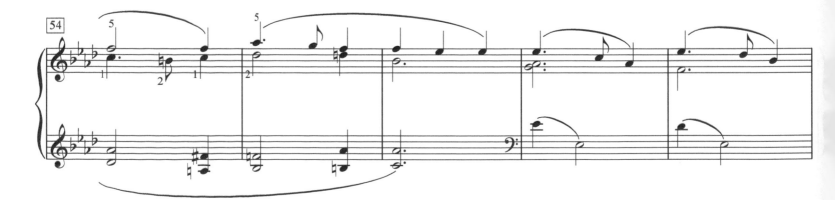

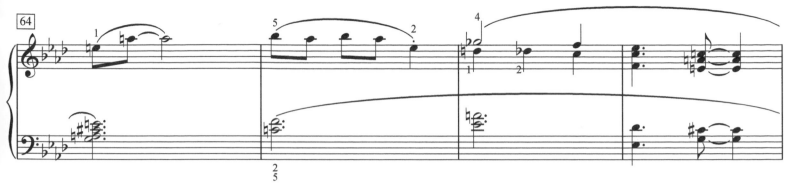

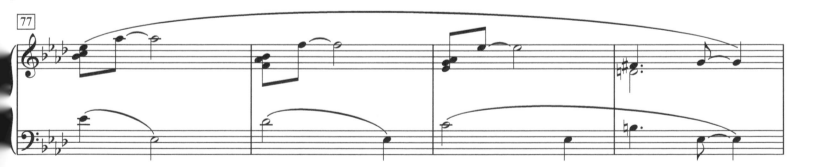

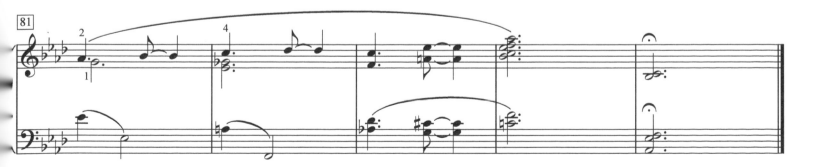

THE SWAN

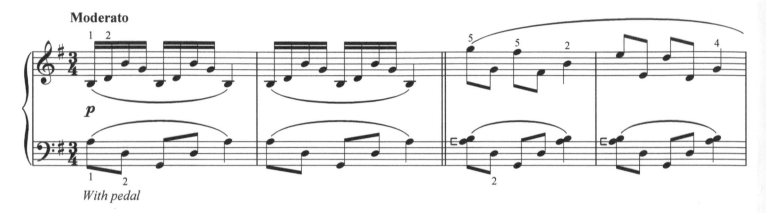

CAMILLE SAINT-SAËNS
Arranged by LEE EVANS

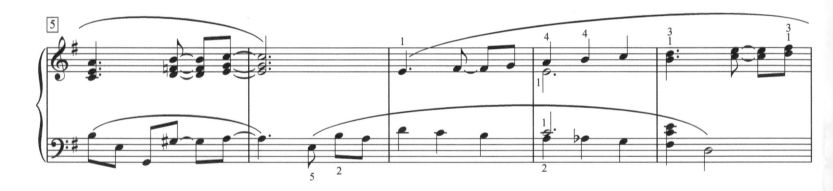

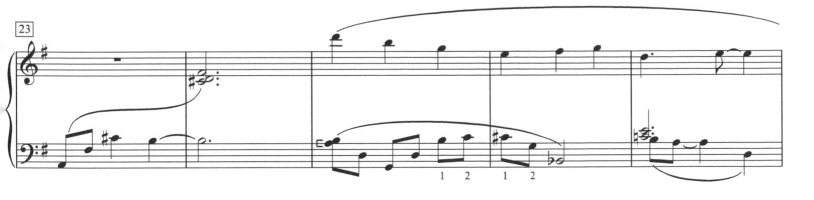

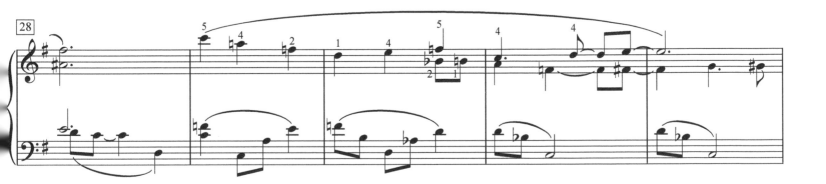

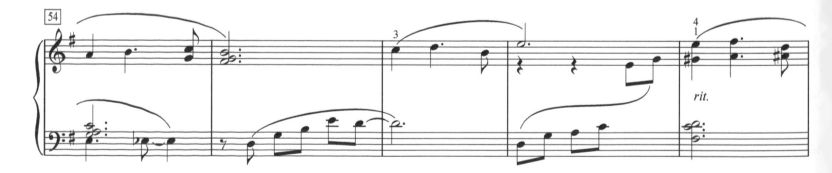

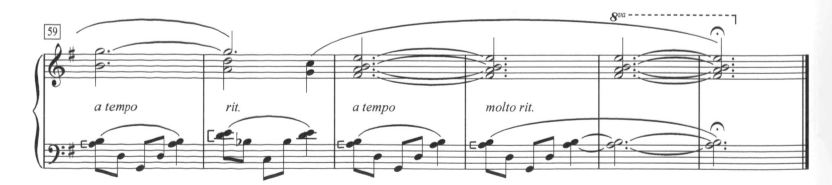

RECUERDOS DE LA ALHAMBRA

FRANCISCO TÁRREGA
Arranged by LEE EVANS

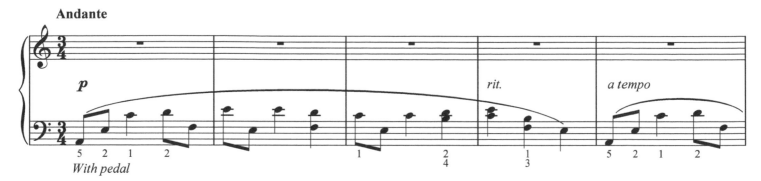

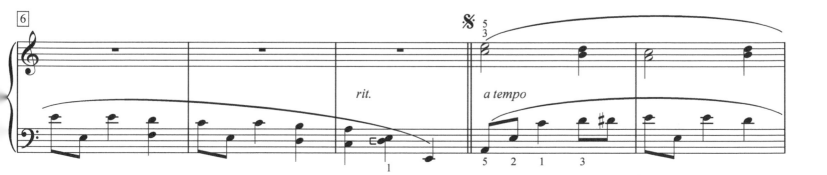

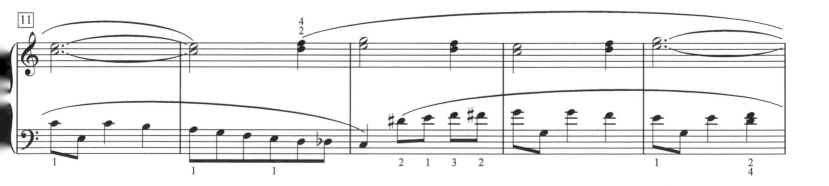

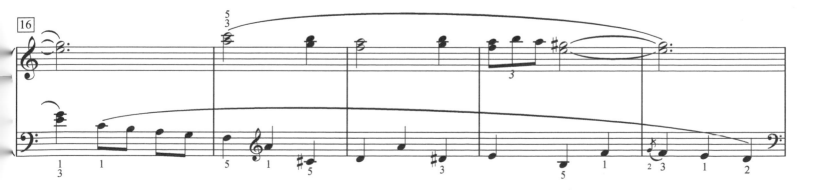

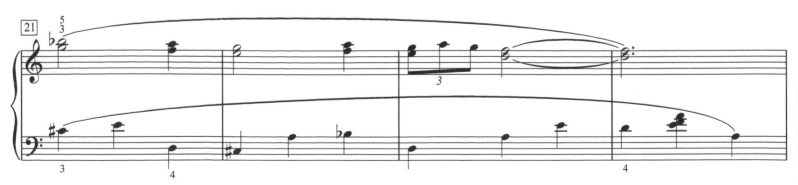

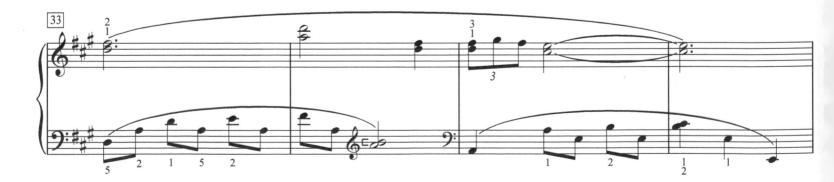

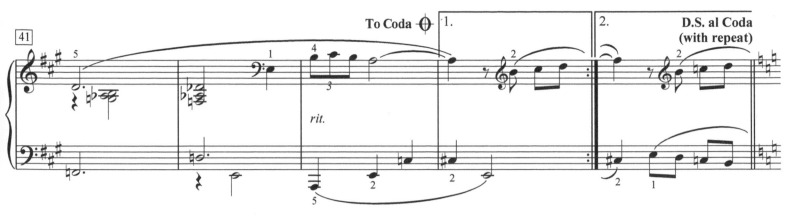

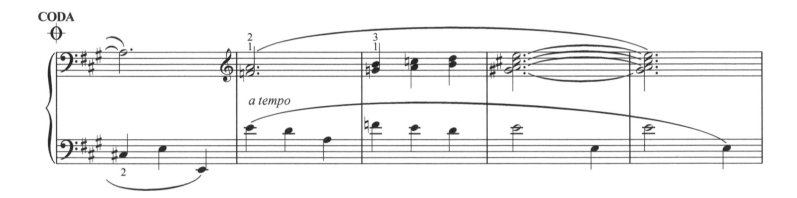

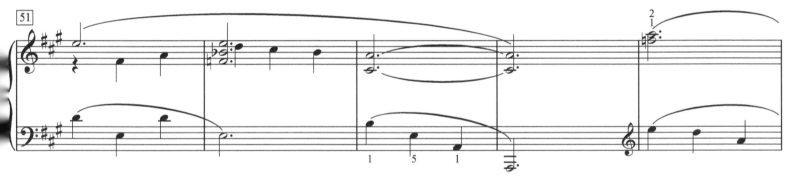

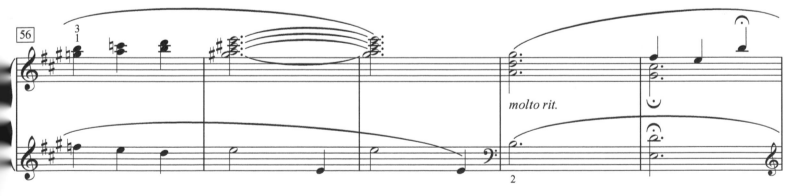

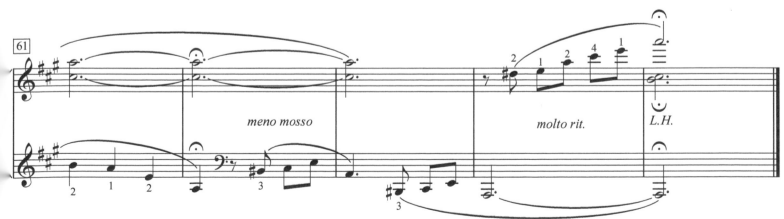

ARIOSO
from CANTATA BWV 156

JOHANN SEBASTIAN BACH
Arranged by LEE EVANS

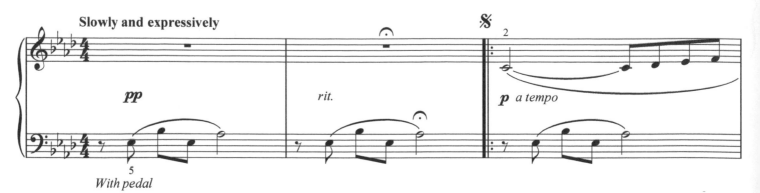

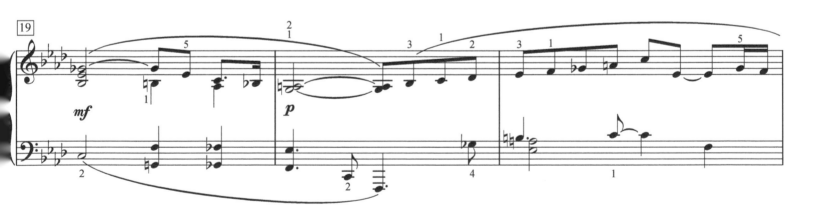

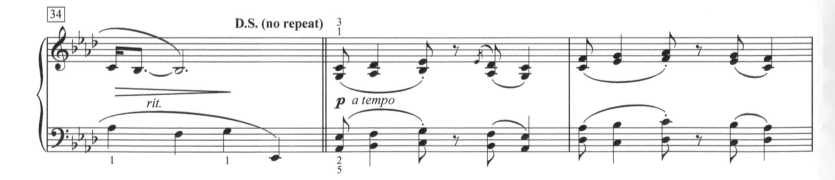

BARCAROLLE
"June" from THE SEASONS, Op. 37, No. 6

PYOTR IL'YICH TCHAIKOVSKY
Arranged by LEE EVANS

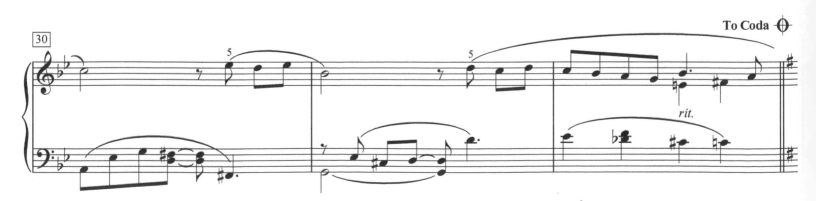

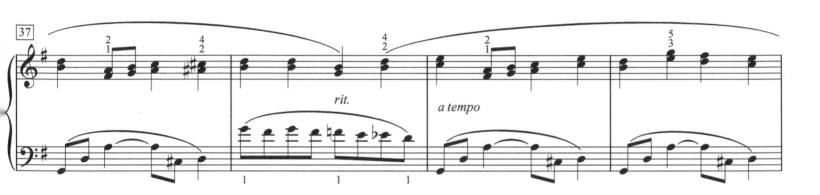

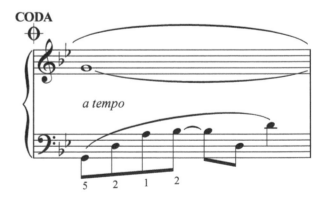

LARGO FROM SYMPHONY NO. 9
("New World")

ANTONIN DVOŘÁK
Arranged by LEE EVANS

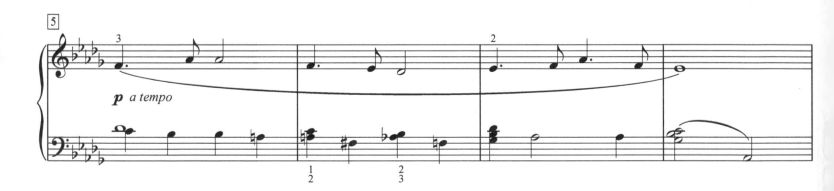

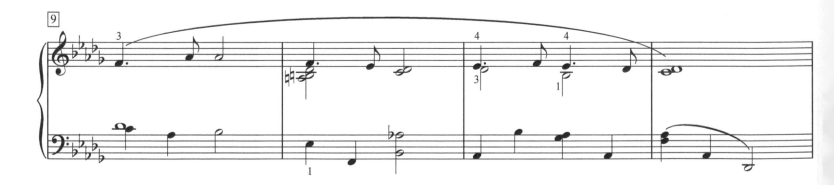

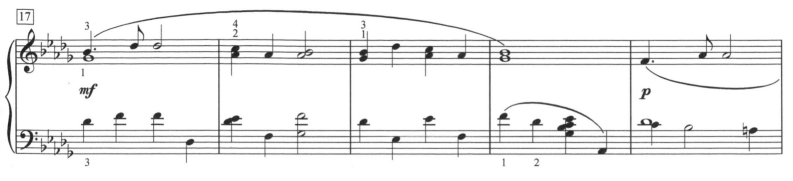

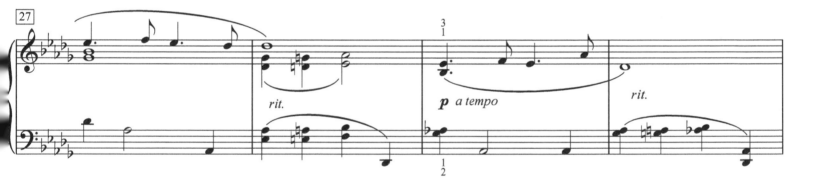

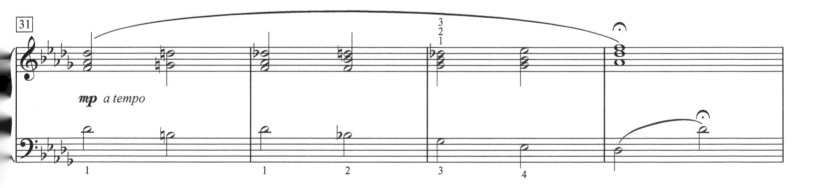

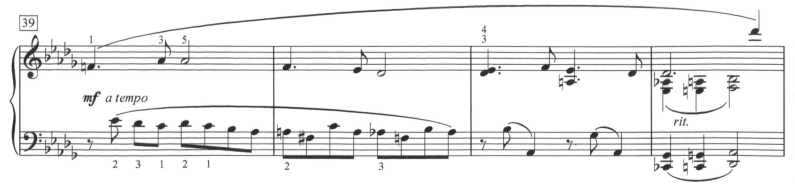

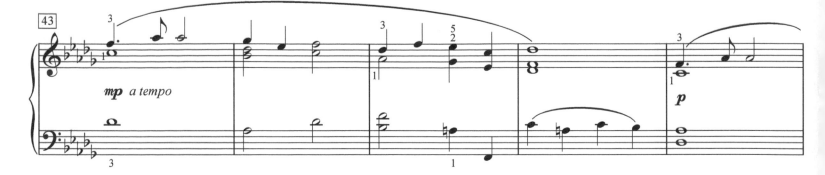

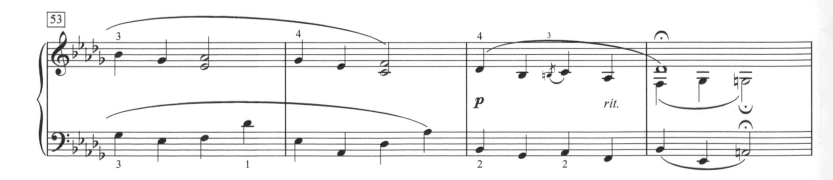

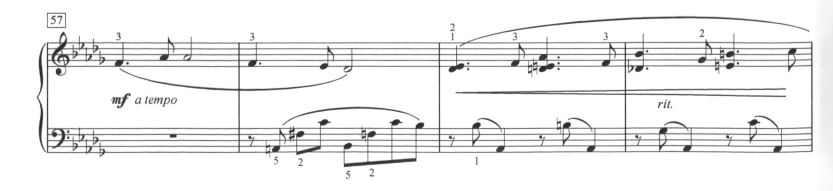

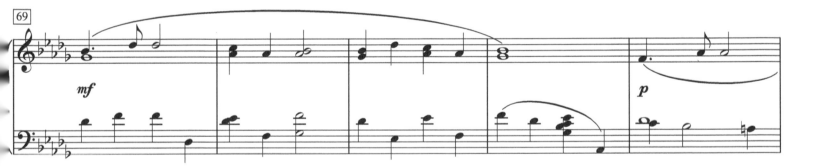

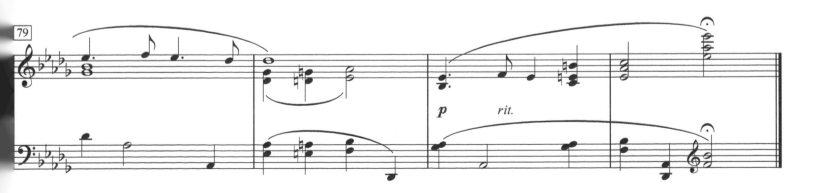

SICILIANO
from Flute Sonata No. 2, BWV 1031

JOHANN SEBASTIAN BACH
Arranged by LEE EVANS

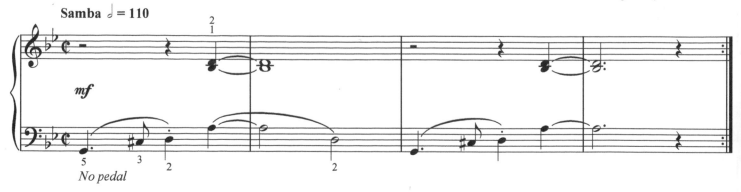

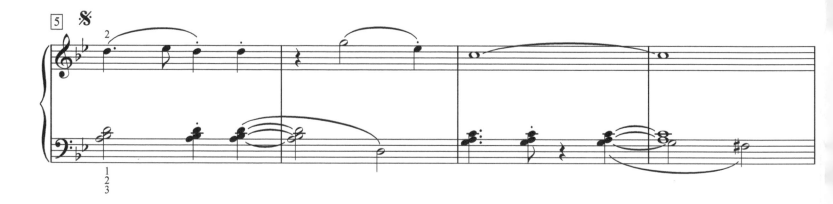

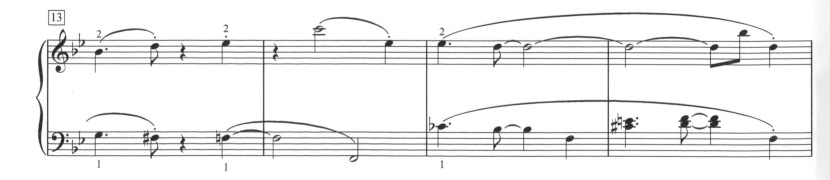

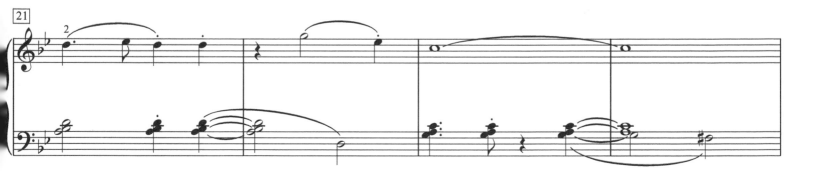

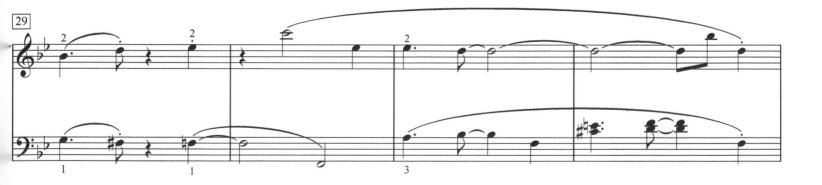

To Coda

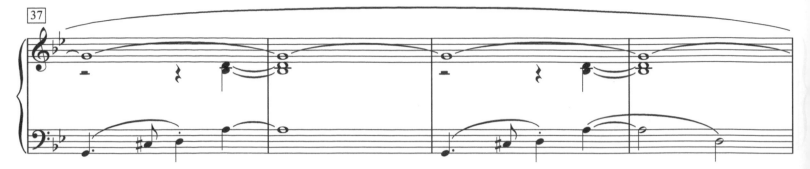

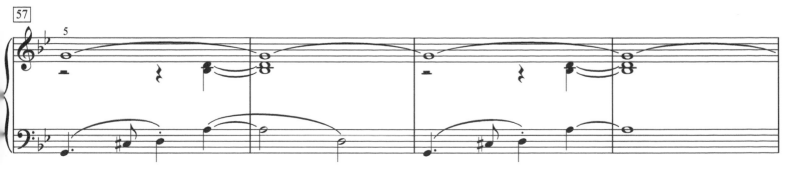

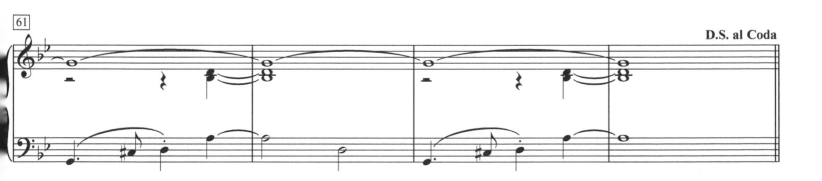

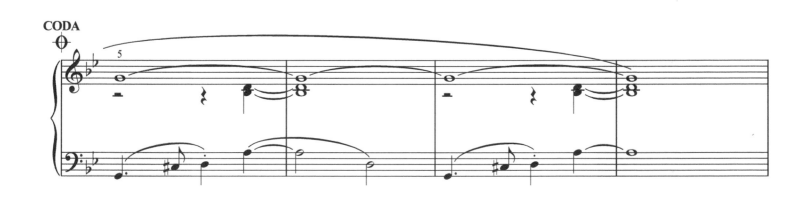

D.S. al Coda

CODA

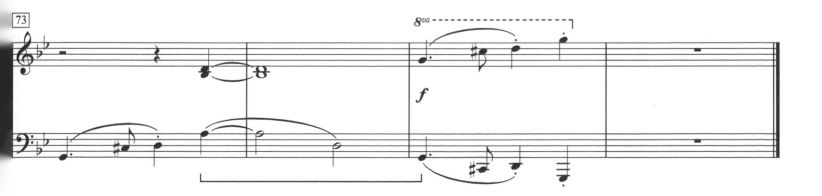

ANDANTE CANTABILE

from String Quartet No. 1, Op. 11, 2nd Movement Theme

PYOTR IL'YICH TCHAIKOVSKY
Arranged by LEE EVANS

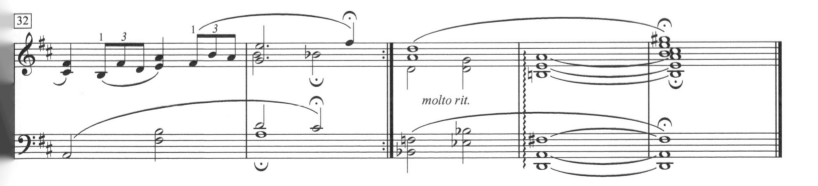

TO A WILD ROSE
Theme and Variations

Rose Theme (Original)

EDWARD MacDOWELL
Arranged by LEE EVANS

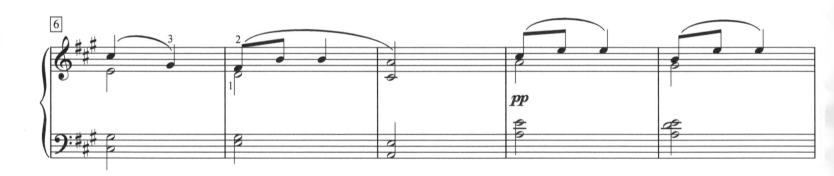

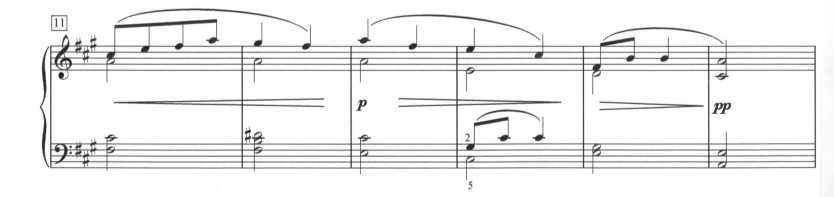

I. Gardenia

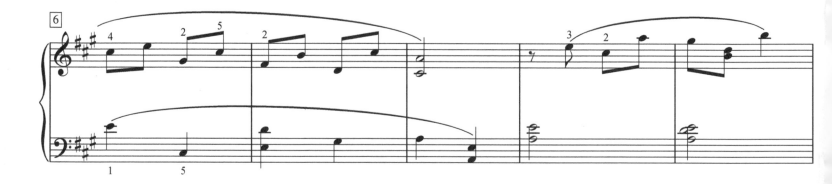

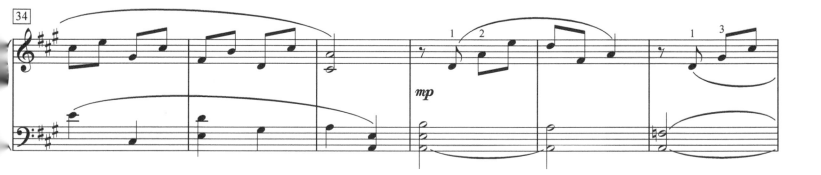

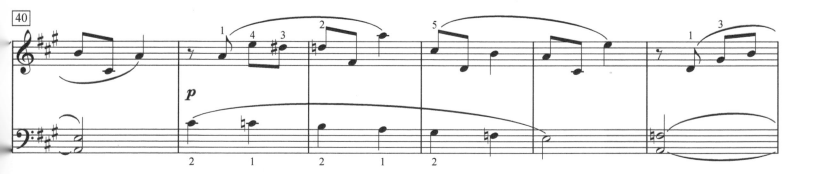

56

II. Bird-of-Paradise

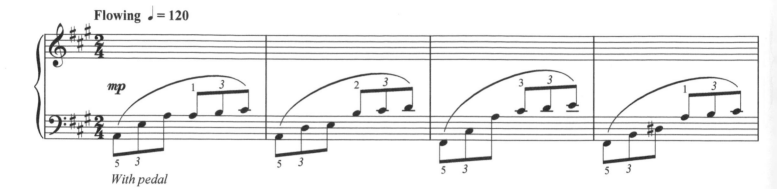

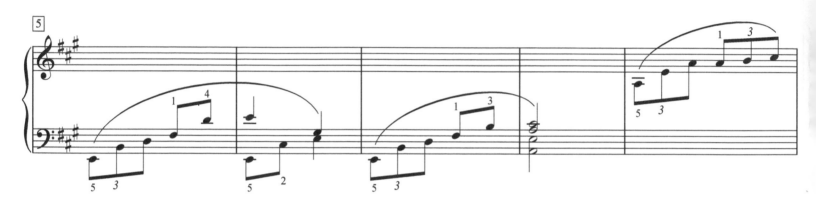

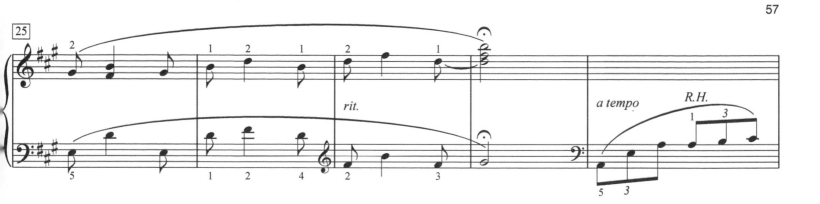

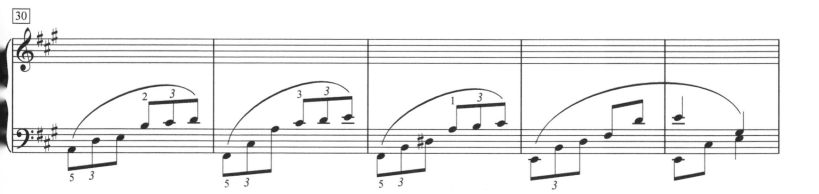

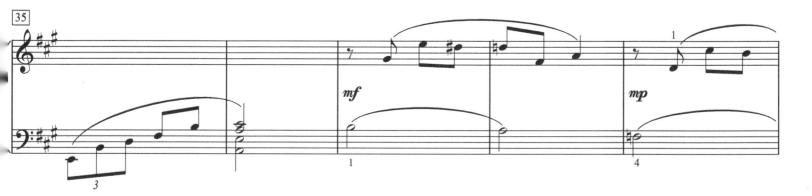

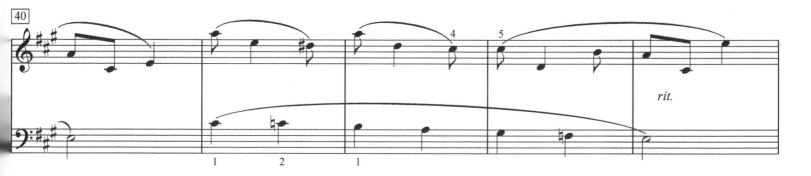

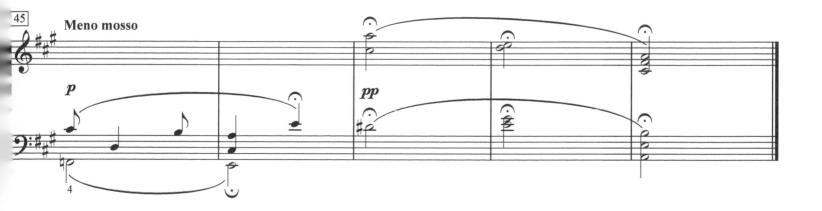

III. Forget-Me-Not

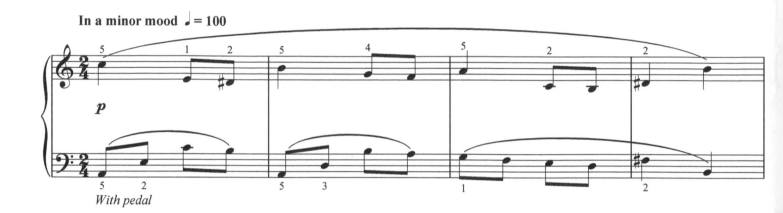

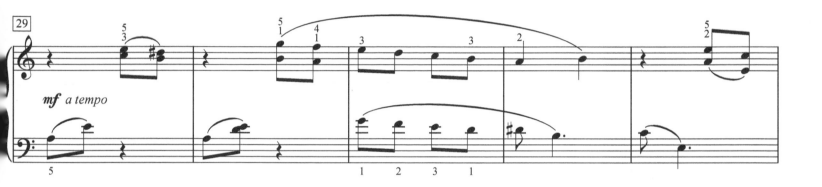

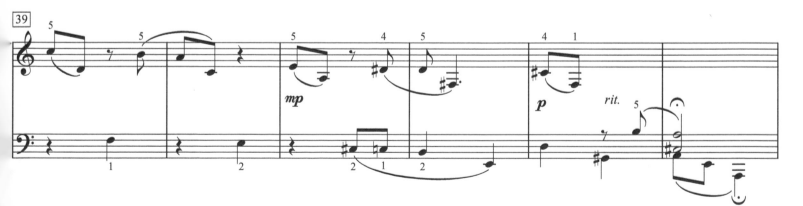

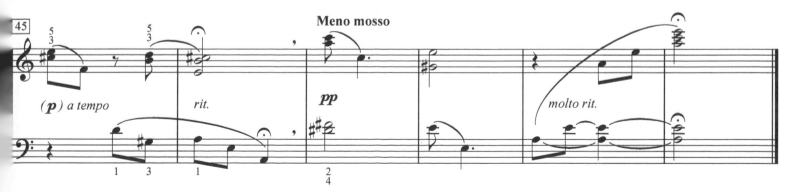

IV. Marigold

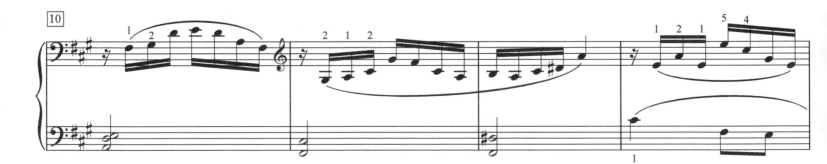

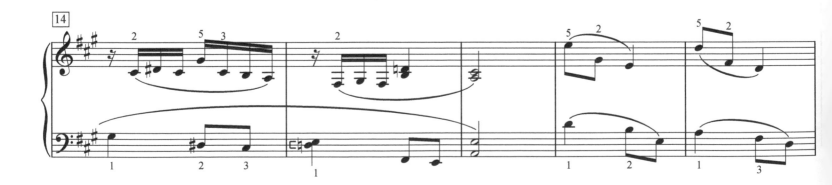

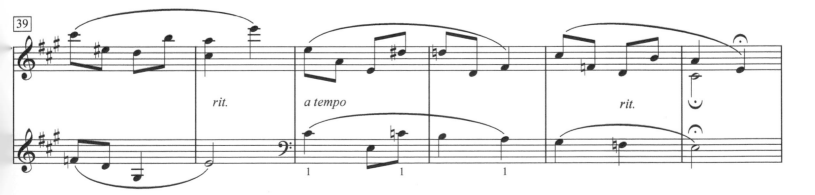

Meno mosso

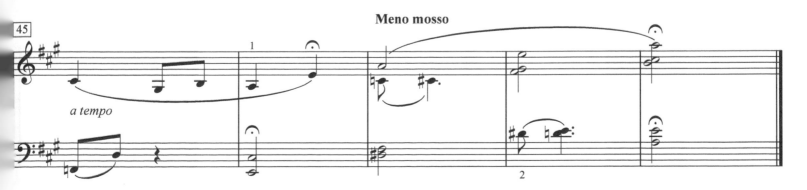

Rose Theme (Reprise)

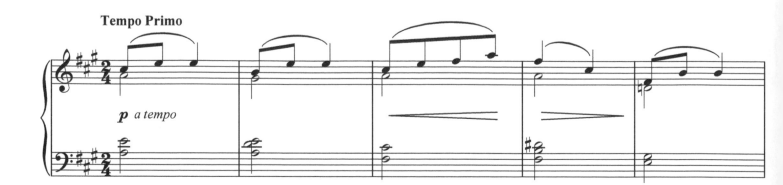

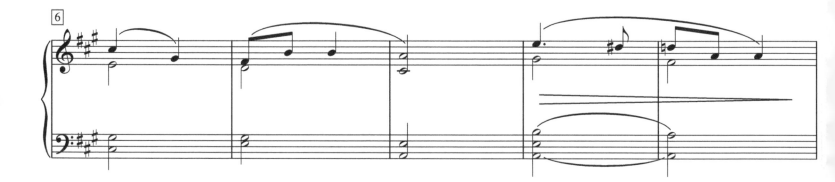

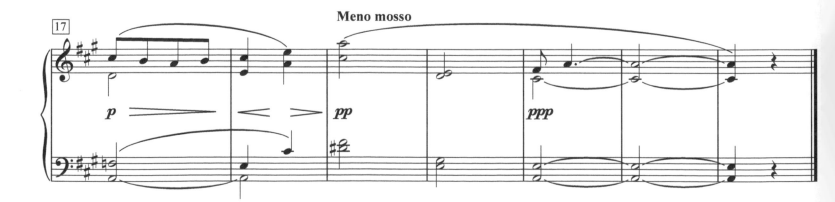

PIANO CONCERTO NO. 23
K. 488, 2nd Movement Theme

WOLFGANG AMADEUS MOZART
Arranged by LEE EVANS

Andante

p

With pedal

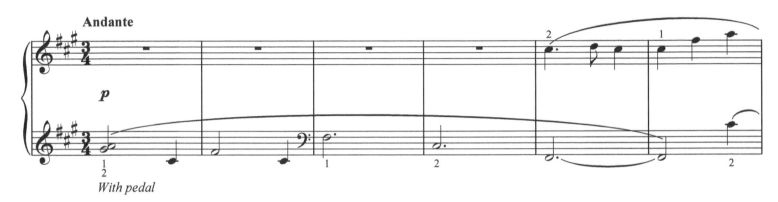

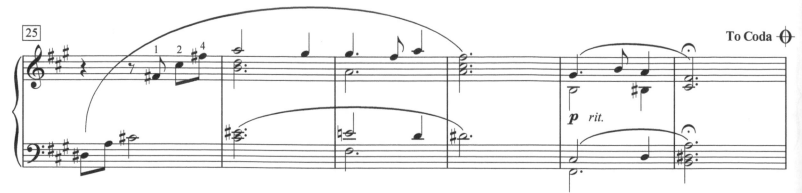

To Coda ⊕

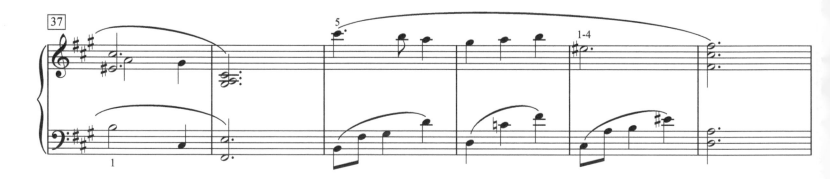

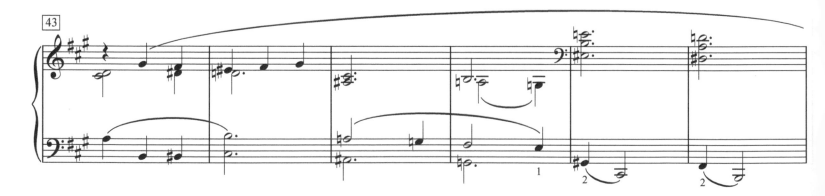

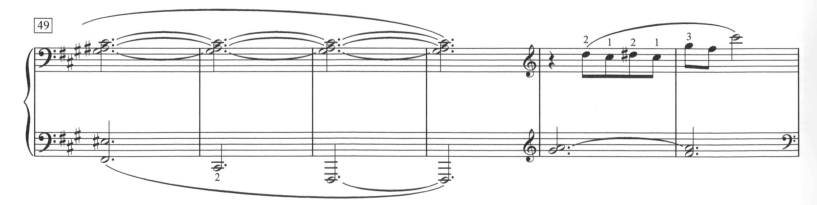

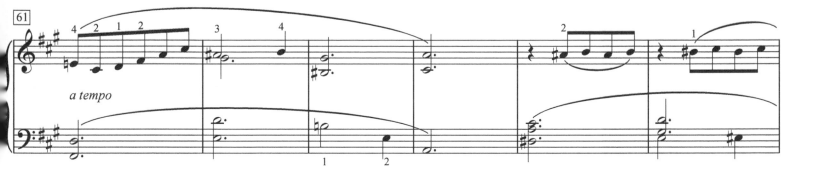

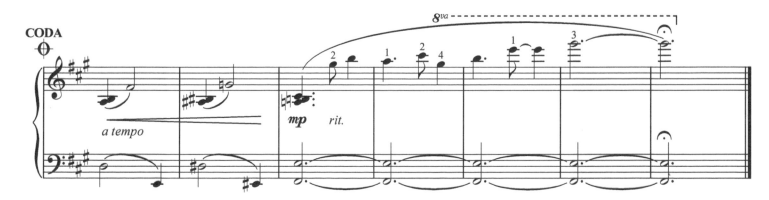

PANIS ANGELICUS
(O Lord Most Holy)

CÉSAR FRANCK
Arranged by LEE EVANS

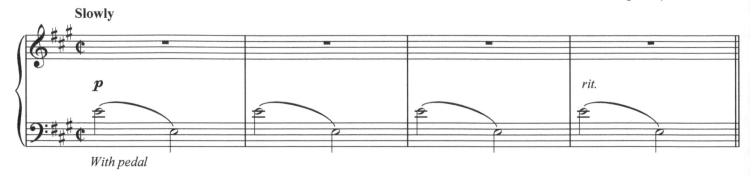

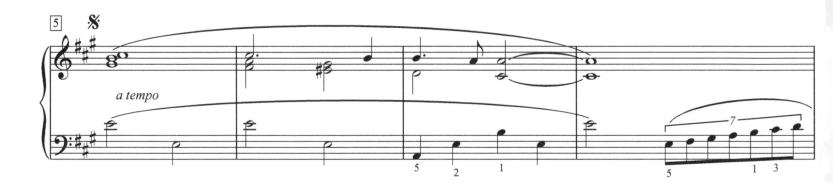

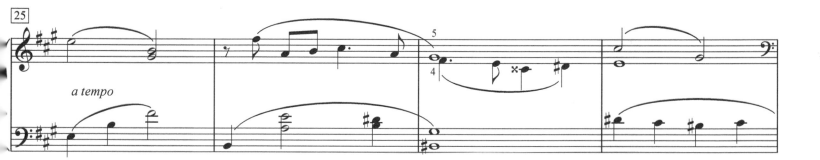

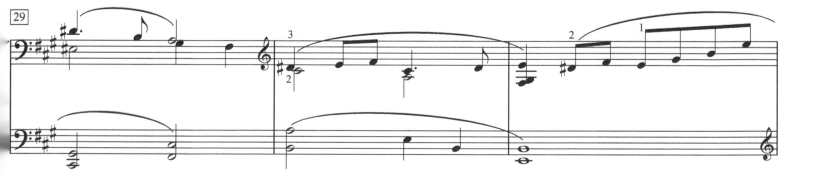

D.S. al Coda

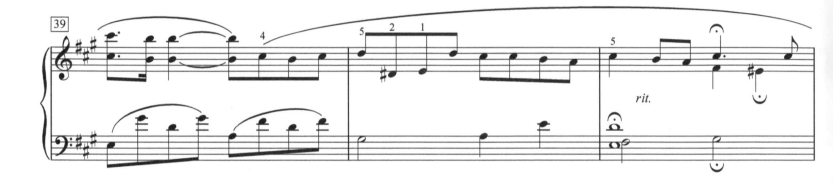

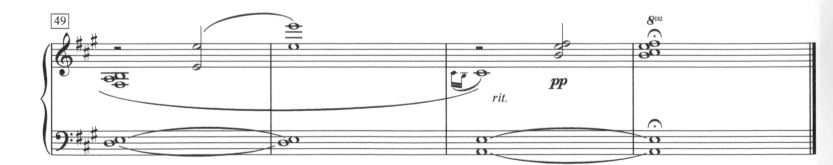

IL LAMENTO DI FEDERICO
from L'ARLESIANA

FRANCESCO CILEA
Arranged by LEE EVANS

Molto sostenuto ♩ = 60

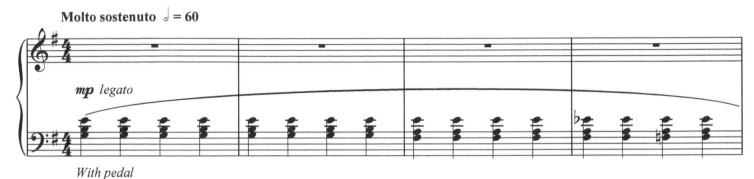

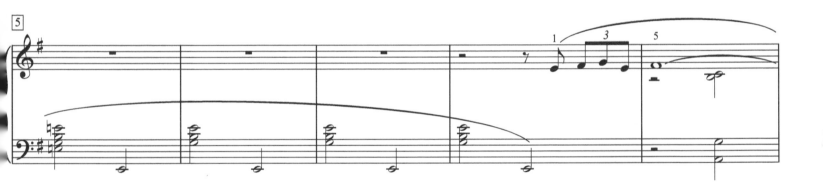

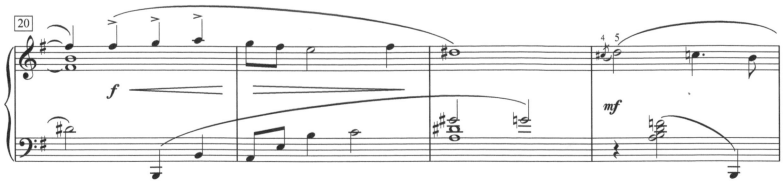

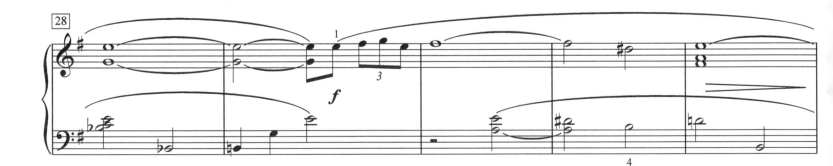

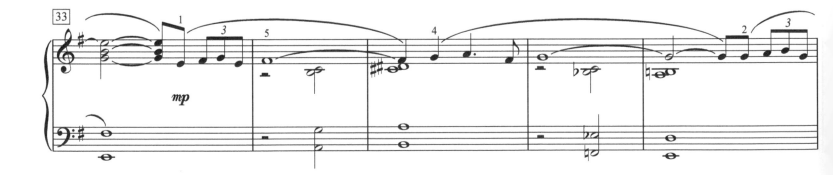

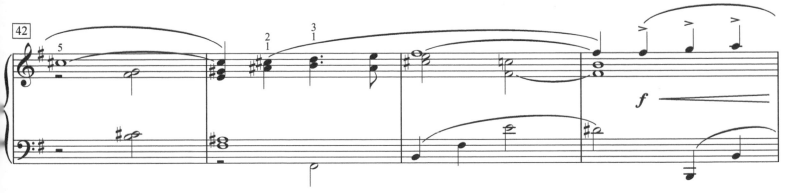

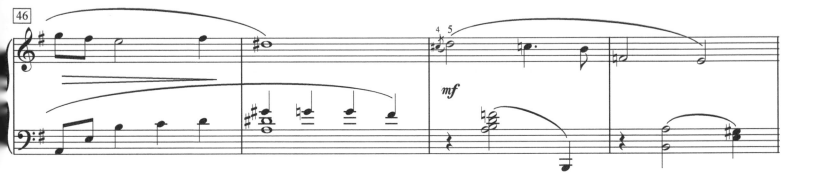

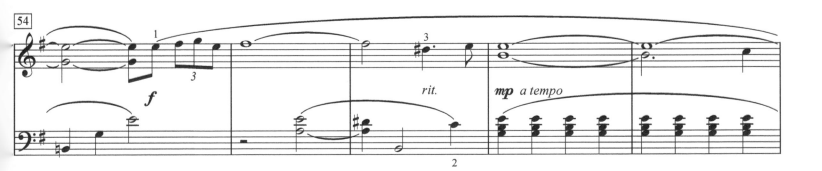

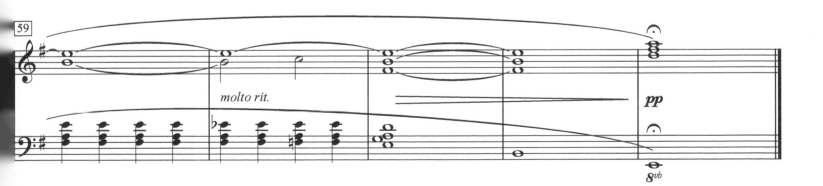

SALUT D'AMOUR
(Greeting to Love)

EDWARD ELGAR
Arranged by LEE EVANS

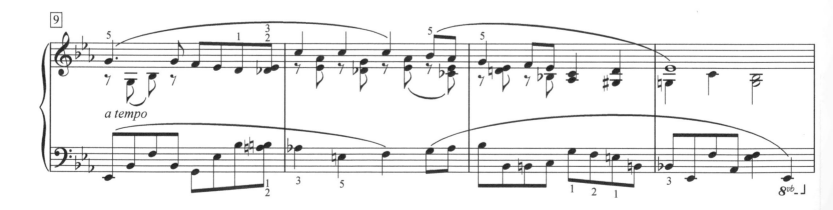

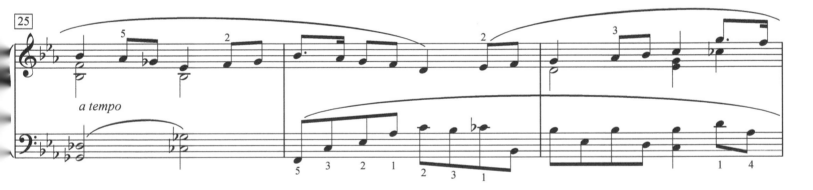

SOLVEIG'S SONG

Poem by HENRIK IBSEN
English version by ARTHUR WESTBROOK
Music by EDVARD GRIEG
Arranged by LEE EVANS

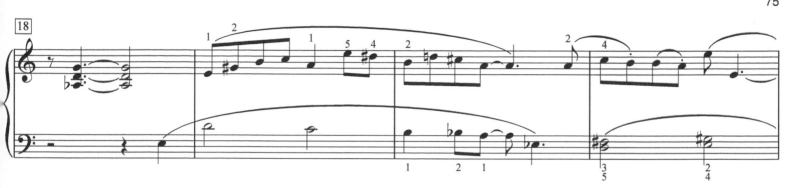

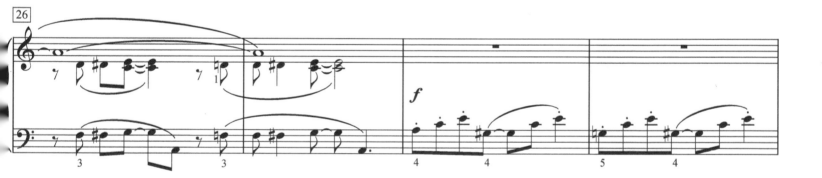

D.C. with repeat

APRÈS UN RÊVE
(After a Dream)

GABRIEL FAURÉ
Arranged by LEE EVANS

Andantino; molto rubato

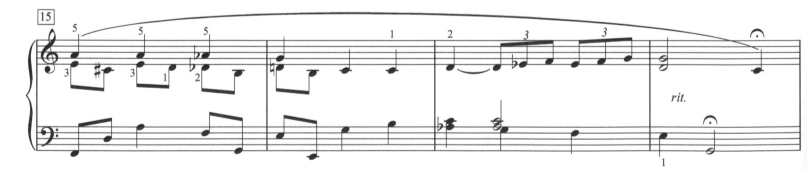

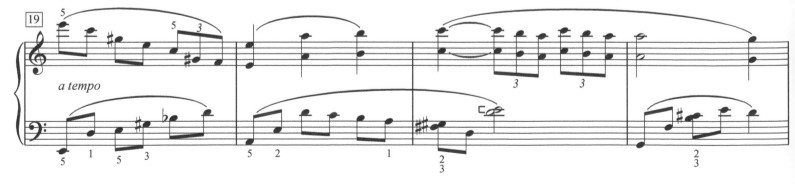

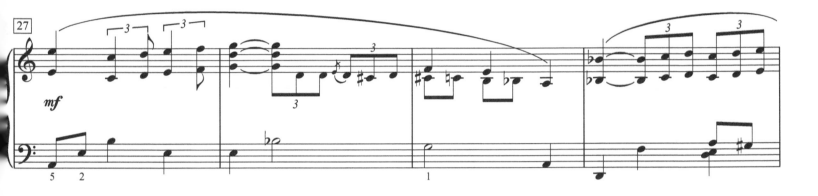

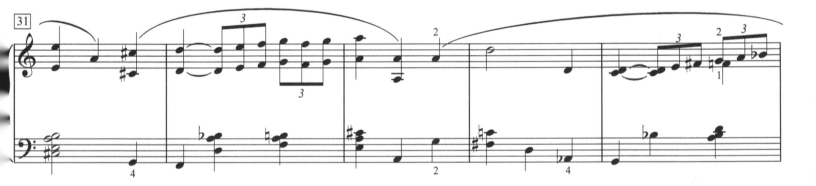

To Coda ⊕

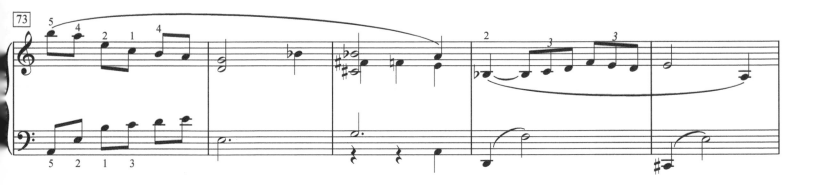

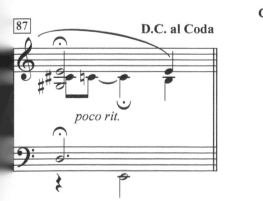

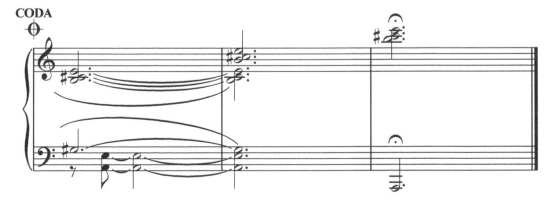

À LA MANIÈRE DE BORODINE
(Valse)

MAURICE RAVEL
Arranged by LEE EVANS

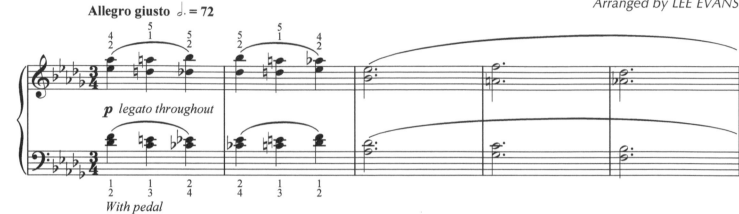

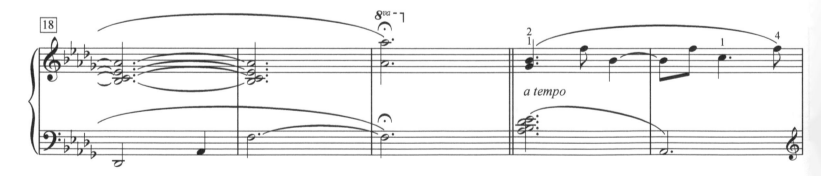

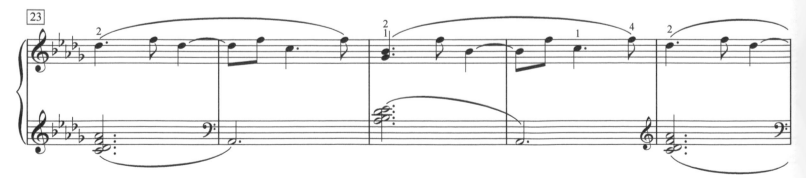

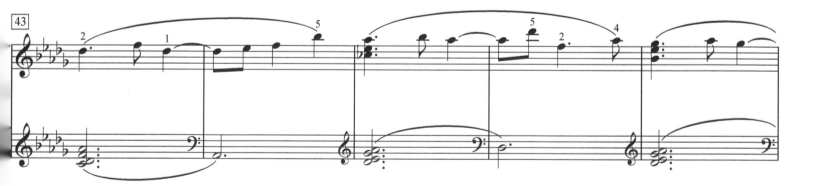

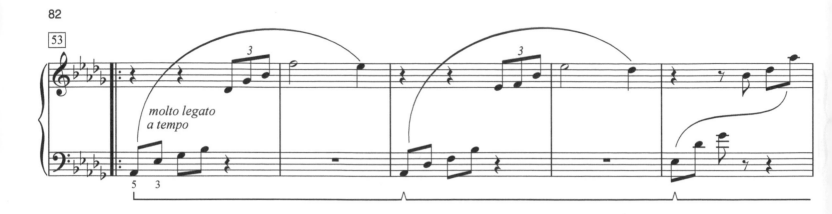

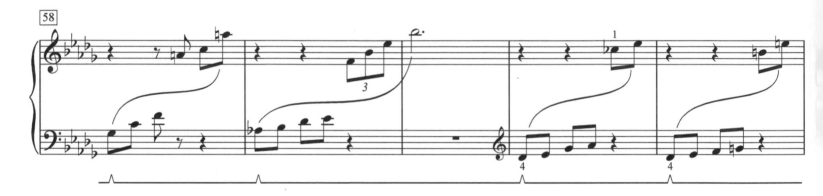

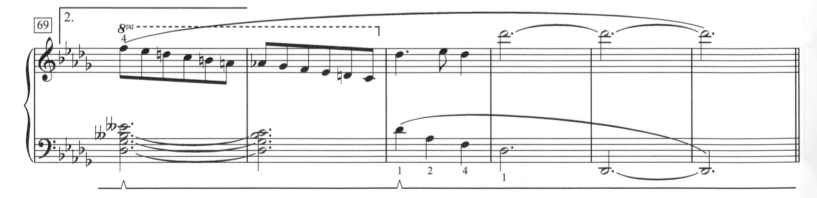

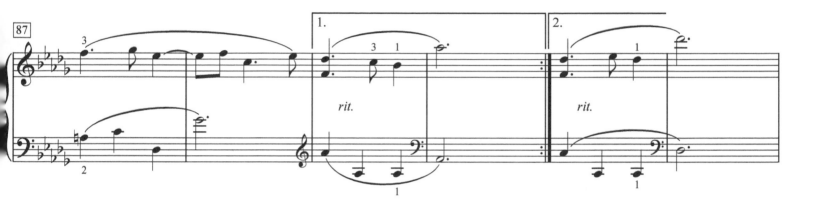

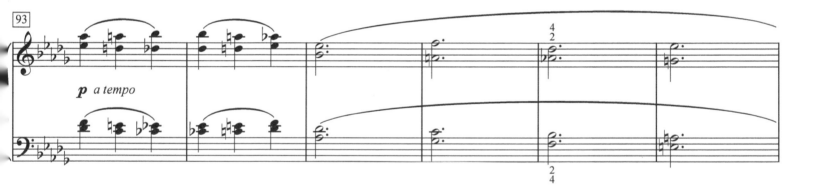

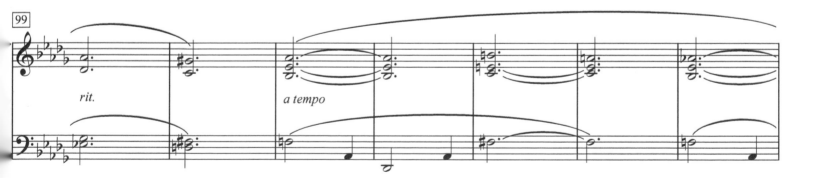

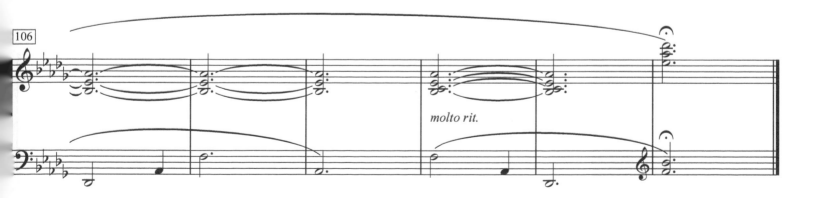

MEDITATION
from THAÏS

JULES MASSENET
Arranged by LEE EVANS

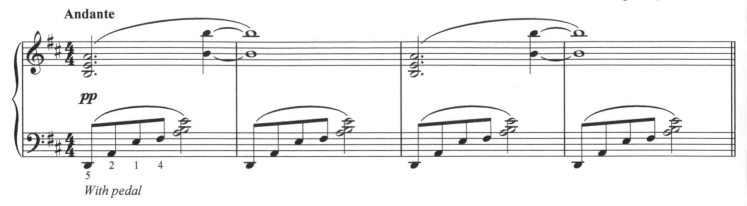

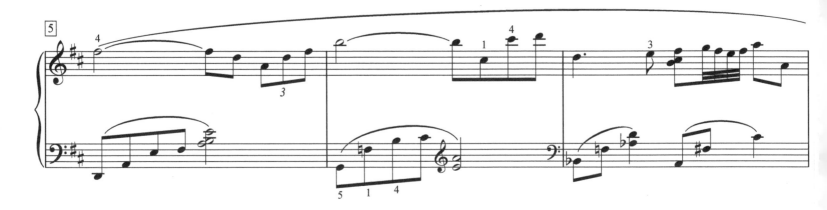

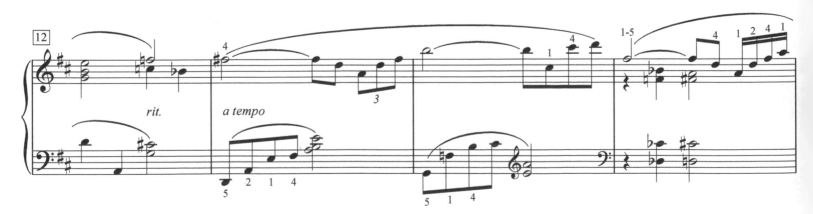

A bit faster

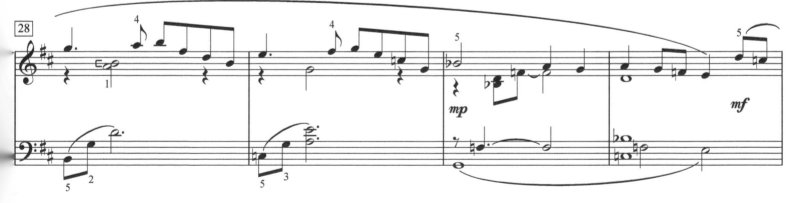

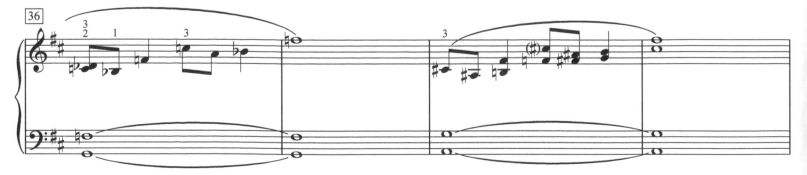

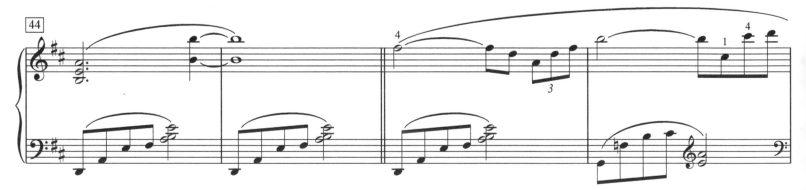

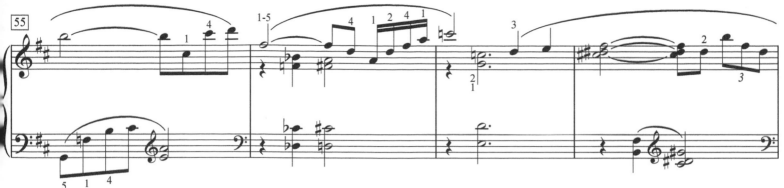

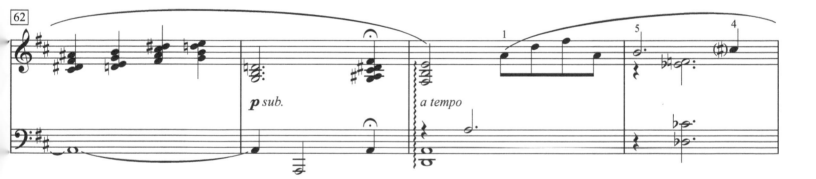

PLAY PIANO LIKE A PRO!

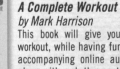